LET'S PLAY I SPY WITH MY LITTLE EYE MOTORBIKES

I SPY ALL

SPORT MOTORBIKES

PIZZA

I SPY ALL

DIRT BIKES

I SPY
ALL

CHOPPERS

I SPY ALL

SCOOTERS

TAXI

I SPY ALL

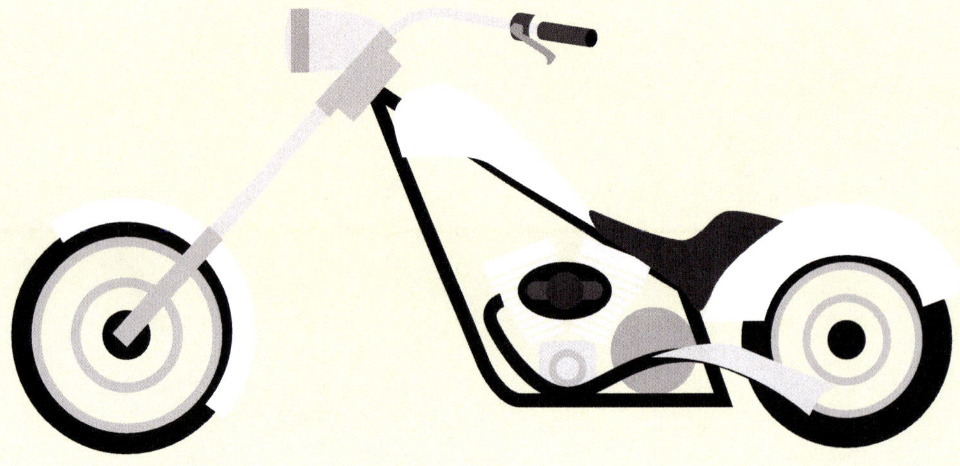

CHOPPERS

I SPY ALL

SPORT MOTORBIKES

I SPY ALL

CLASSIC MOTORBIKES

I SPY ALL

DIRT MOTORBIKES

TAXI
TAXI

I SPY ALL

SCOOTERS

I SPY ALL

RACE MOTORBIKES

RACING

I SPY ALL

CLASSIC MOTORBIKES

I SPY ALL

SCOOTERS

EMERGENCY

I SPY ALL

ORANGE SCOOTERS

TAXI

I SPY ALL

RACING MOTORBIKES

TAXI
POLICE

Made in the USA
Middletown, DE
12 January 2024